VISITING ANNE'S HOUSE

BY ELAINE ROCHE-TOMBEE
ILLUSTRATED BY MARY BOLLINGER

CHAPTERS

Fact or Fiction? 2

The Author and Anne 5

Not Just Books 9

The Anne Tour 13

Harcourt

Orlando   Boston   Dallas   Chicago   San Diego

Visit *The Learning Site!*

www.harcourtschool.com

FACT OR FICTION?

Her name was Anne Shirley. She had bright-red hair and a terrible temper. She was quick to become upset if you spelled her name without the *e*. She often used big words, causing people to look bewildered. Still, people have found her irresistible for nearly a hundred years.

Anne grew up in Avonlea, on Canada's Prince Edward Island. Visitors today tour Green Gables, the house where she lived. They walk the paths of this small community that has changed little since Anne's day.

There's one thing wrong with this picture—well, actually, several things. Anne Shirley never lived in Avonlea. In fact, there is no Avonlea, and Anne never lived at all. She is a fictional character. She first appeared in *Anne of Green Gables*, a book by Lucy Maud Montgomery.

Even so, tourists flock to the town "where Anne grew up." They peep into Anne's room. They dress up in Anne's clothes. They laugh at the cracked writing slate that Anne broke over the head of a boy who teased her. They solemnly exchange wedding vows by a special fireplace. Anne's creator was married by this fireplace, but Anne was not.

Anne's fans find the experience sublime. Yet people who have never read *Anne of Green Gables* are often bewildered. How did the home of a made-up person become a tourist attraction?

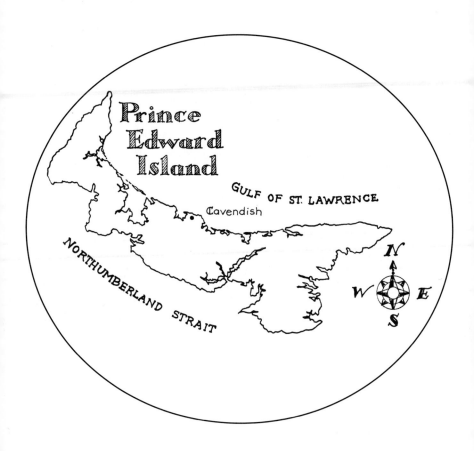

Prince Edward Island is Canada's smallest province. There is no Avonlea, but there is a town called Cavendish on the island's north shore.

THE AUTHOR AND ANNE

Lucy Maud Montgomery was born on Prince Edward Island in 1874. She was raised by her grandparents in Cavendish. Montgomery attended college and later taught school and worked for a newspaper. She also wrote poems and stories. In 1908 she published *Anne of Green Gables*, her first novel.

In the book, the aging bachelor Matthew Cuthbert and his sister Marilla send for an orphan child. They want a child to help out on their farm. This part of the story is based on fact.

From 1850 to 1920, "orphan trains" brought more than 150,000 children from the East Coast to the Midwest and the West. The children were given to families that asked for them. Some of the families wanted children to care for and to love. Some wanted unpaid help.

The children on the trains came from crowded cities in the East. Not all of them were orphans. Some had families that simply could not care for them. Other children were homeless and had lived on the street.

In the story, the Cuthberts are expecting a strong boy to help with chores. Instead, they get a girl—eleven-year-old Anne.

At first, Anne tends to fluster the Cuthberts.
Marilla wants to send her back, but Anne soon wins
them over. They grow to love her imagination and
sunny personality. In time, she brightens the lives of
the people of Avonlea dramatically.

Anne of Green Gables was an immediate success
in Canada and the United States. To understand why,
you might read the other children's books of the early
1900s. They tended to preach solemnly at their readers. When we read these books today, their characters
seem false.

Anne, in contrast, was fun and playful. Her approach to life made her irresistible. She faced the world with courage and honesty. Like a real child, Anne wanted to find her place in the world. Adults also liked her sense of responsibility toward others.

In writing *Anne*, Montgomery drew on her own experiences. Cavendish became Avonlea. Its people became Anne's neighbors. The Cuthberts' house, Green Gables, was modeled on the home of Montgomery's cousins.

Anne of Green Gables continues to be popular. It has never been out of print. This novel has sold more than nine million copies and has been translated into seventeen languages. *Anne of Avonlea*, the first of five additional books about Anne, appeared in 1909. These five books tell about Anne's career, marriage, and family.

NOT JUST BOOKS

The first movie based on *Anne of Green Gables* came out in 1919. Several others followed. Before making a movie that came out in 1985, the director traveled across Canada. He was searching for just the right actor to play Anne. He interviewed more than 3,000 girls. Finally, he chose a 16-year-old from Toronto.

The Anne Books

Three TV serials have been based on the *Anne* books. The 1985 version was Canada's most-watched TV series ever.

In all, Lucy Maud Montgomery wrote more than twenty books. In addition to the six books about Anne, she wrote two novels about Anne's "daughter." She also wrote two novels about another orphan, Emily Byrd Starr. The titles are *Emily of New Moon* and *Emily's Quest*.

In 1935, Lucy Montgomery received the Order of the British Empire for her contributions to children's literature. She died in 1942.

The town of Cavendish, population 196, now hosts hundreds of thousands of visitors each year. Green Gables and its grounds have been lovingly restored in great detail. The furniture is from the early 1900s. Visitors can also find items suggested by the *Anne* books, such as the cracked slate.

In 1999, the Avonlea Village in Cavendish opened to visitors. Some of the buildings are new. They were built to look like the ones on Prince Edward Island one hundred years ago. Other buildings were moved to the village from their original sites. One of them is the schoolhouse where Lucy Montgomery once taught.

"Anne" and her best friend "Diana" are often seen in the village. Guests enjoy musical entertainment in the evenings.

The Anne Tour

The "Anne tour" includes a ride in "Matthew's buggy." A horse draws the carriage around the pond that Anne's imagination turned into the "Lake of Shining Waters."

At the Anne of Green Gables Store, tourists buy Anne dolls. They tour the factory where the dolls are made. They buy Anne books and Anne hats, even Anne snacks. They explore the forest Anne described. They walk down the cow path she followed.

Anne's story is dramatically portrayed in *Anne of Green Gables: The Musical*. The play has run on Prince Edward Island every summer since 1965.

Another show is called *Anne and Diana*. Audiences laugh as Diana becomes annoyed with Anne's temper. They smile as Anne begs for forgiveness. The play is part of a Lucy Maud Montgomery Festival held every August.

Visitors from Japan are among Anne's greatest fans. *Anne of Green Gables* was translated into Japanese in 1954. Japanese children read it as part of their middle-school program. Many young Japanese women read the book again when applying for jobs. They hope to be inspired by Anne's honesty and courage.

A full-sized model of the Green Gables house stands in a Japanese theme park. There are Anne cartoons on Japanese TV. The Anne Academy teaches English to its students.

A Japanese travel magazine once asked its readers what places they would most like to visit. The leading vote-getters were New York, Paris, and London. In fourth place was Prince Edward Island.

All of the attention Anne receives might fluster even her. Then again, perhaps she would be delighted to know she has so many fans.

Of course, she would probably call them "kindred spirits."